Alone, Awakened and Alive

OrangeBooks Publication

1st Floor, Rajhans Arcade, Mall Road, Kohka, Bhilai, Chhattisgarh 490020
Website: **www.orangebooks.in**

First Edition, 2025

ISBN: 978-93-6554-352-0

Price: Rs. 299.00

Printed in India

Alone Awakened And Alive

RECLAIMING POWER, PURPOSE & PEACE ON YOUR SOLO JOURNEY

"Alone, Awakened, and Alive is Smithaa's gift to every soul who has ever felt incomplete - reminding us that wholeness, peace and power is always within us, we just need to find it."

- Ms. SUSHMITA SEN, ACTOR, PHILANTHROPIST & MISS UNIVERSE 1994

SMITHAA M CHATURVEDI

OrangeBooks Publication

www.orangebooks.in

To the graceful and inspiring

Sushmita Sen

Dear Ms. Sushmita Sen,

Thank you so much for your incredible endorsement of my book. Your words are truly a gift, and I am so grateful for the time and thought you put into reading and sharing your perspective on my work.

Your support means the world to me. As someone who has long admired your grace, intelligence, and independence, having your name associated with my book is a profound honor. I hope that your endorsement will inspire many more readers to connect with the book and learn from it.

Thank you once again for your kindness and generosity.

With heartfelt gratitude,
Smithaa M Chaturvedi

Dedication

I bow down in gratitude to Shiva, my Sakha Kanha and all my Gurus, Spirit Guides and Ancestors who are always by my side and continue to support and protect me on my journey.

I would like to dedicate this book to my parents Late Mr. Murarilal Chaturvedi (Dad) and Late Mrs. Rajkumari Chaturvedi (Mom) who always faced challenges with a smile and a song and taught me to be a fighter and never give up in the face of adversities

My deepest gratitude to all those people who contributed directly or indirectly towards making me the strong, empowered, healed and awakened woman I am today.

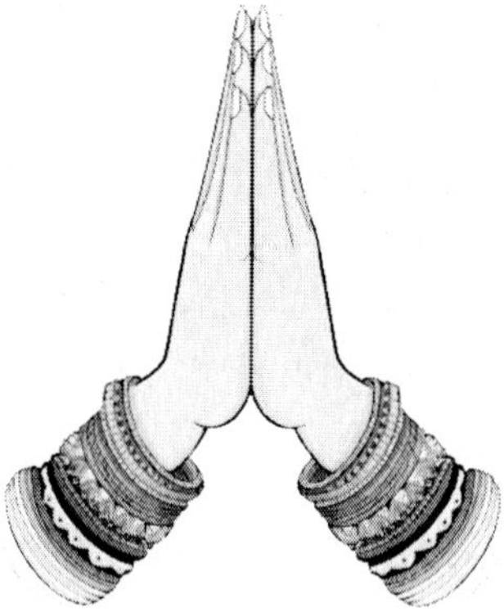

Alone, Awakened and Alive

Reclaiming Power, Purpose and Peace on Your Solo Journey

Introduction:

Embracing the Power of Being Single

There was a time when being single was viewed as a temporary phase — a waiting room for the "real" journey of life to begin. Society often romanticises the idea of partnership, making it seem as though true happiness and fulfilment can only be achieved when you find "the one." But what if the most important relationship you will ever have is the one you have with yourself?

Being single is not a flaw or a void that needs to be filled— it is an opportunity. It is a space for self-discovery, personal growth, and complete freedom. It is a chance to design your life exactly the way you want it, without compromise. Whether you are single by choice or by circumstance, this phase of life holds immense potential for you to create the most meaningful and empowering relationship of all — the one with yourself.

The Stigma of Being Single

Let's face it — the world often glorifies coupledom. Social media feeds are filled with romantic getaways, weddings, and anniversary celebrations. Movies and books frequently push the narrative that love is the ultimate goal. As a result, being single can sometimes feel like you are missing out or falling behind.

But here is the truth: You are not incomplete because you are single. Your worth is not determined by your relationship status. You are whole on your own.

Why This Book?

Being single for 20 years now, I have seen all the fears, obstacles and problems that could arise when you live alone and have managed to make my life meaningful. I would like to share my experience and learnings to help people going through the same. This book is not about helping you "survive" singlehood as if it were a problem. It is about thriving in it. It is about shifting your mindset from seeing singleness as an absence to viewing it as a powerful, fulfilling presence. Through these pages, you will learn to embrace your independence, conquer moments of loneliness, and build a vibrant life that you love — whether or not you ever find a partner

You Will Discover How To:

- Cultivate self-love and confidence.
- Enjoy your own company without feeling lonely.
- Build meaningful friendships and social connections.
- Heal from past heartbreaks and prepare for future relationships.
- Thrive emotionally, mentally, and financially as a single person.

Alone, but Not Lonely

Being alone does not have to mean being lonely. Loneliness is a state of mind, not a relationship status. It can strike people in partnerships just as easily as those who are single. The difference lies in how you relate to yourself. This book will empower you with the tools and mindset shifts you need to find contentment and joy in your own presence.

The Beauty of Being Unapologetically You

When you are single, you have the freedom to explore, experiment, and redefine yourself. You can take spontaneous trips, dive into new hobbies, and build a life that reflects your true desires — without compromise. This is your chance to design a life that brings you fulfilment, happiness, and freedom, regardless of whether or not you share it with a partner.

So, as you turn the pages of this book, remember: you are not waiting for someone to complete you — you are already whole. And the most beautiful love story you will ever write is the one you create with yourself.

Your journey to an empowered, joyful singlehood begins now.

Content

Chapter - 1

Redefining Singleness – From Lack to Liberation

"You are not a half looking for your other half. You are already whole."

The Misconception of Singleness

For far too long, singleness has been unfairly portrayed as a temporary or undesirable state — a limbo before "real" life begins with a partner. Society frequently views single people with pity, as though they are incomplete or missing out. Family members often ask, *"When are you settling down?"* or *"Haven't you found someone yet?"* as if your happiness is on hold until you are in a relationship. They even ignore or mistreat you at functions and weddings.

But the truth is, singleness is not a period of waiting — it is a period of *being*. It is a valid and complete phase of life, just as meaningful as being in a relationship. In fact, for many people, it can be the most liberating and fulfilling time of their lives.

Singleness does not mean you are "less than." It means you have the freedom to create a life that aligns entirely with your values, passions, and goals — without compromise.

The Liberation of Being Single

When you are single, you have a rare and precious gift: *freedom*. You are free to prioritise your dreams, passions, and personal growth without the need to constantly consider someone else's needs. This is not selfishness — it is self-exploration.

You can:

- Travel spontaneously without needing to consult or accommodate a partner.
- Pursue career goals with full dedication.
- Explore new hobbies or skills without compromise.
- Make major life decisions based solely on what feels right for you.
- Discover and nurture your true self without external influence.

Singleness is not a punishment — it is an invitation to become your most authentic self.

Breaking Free from the "When I Have a Partner" Mindset

It is easy to fall into the trap of postponing happiness until you find a partner. You may tell yourself:

- *"When I have someone, I'll finally travel."*
- *"Once I'm in a relationship, I'll focus on building a home."*
- *"When I find love, I'll feel more complete and worthy."*

But why wait? Your life does not begin with a relationship — it is happening right now. The more you embrace the present moment, the more empowered and fulfilled you will become.

Imagine building a life so rich, so full, and so meaningful on your own that a future relationship (if it comes) is simply a bonus — not a requirement for your happiness.

The Gift of Self-Discovery

When you are single, you have the unique opportunity to turn inward. You can ask yourself questions like:

- *What truly makes me happy?*
- *What are my personal goals and dreams?*
- *What kind of lifestyle do I genuinely desire?*
- *What are my values, and how do I want to live by them?*

Being in a relationship often blurs these lines because you naturally make compromises. But when you are single, you get to know yourself deeply and authentically. You gain clarity about what you want and what you stand for.

Thriving in Your Own Company

Learning to enjoy your own company is one of the most empowering skills you can develop. When you can sit alone with yourself — without distraction or discomfort — you become emotionally self-reliant.

Ways to cultivate self-enjoyment:

- **Go on solo dates:** Take yourself out for dinner, visit a museum, or watch a movie alone. Learn to cherish your own presence.
- **Practice solo hobbies:** Painting, hiking, cooking, or dancing — explore activities that bring you joy on your own.
- **Create personal rituals:** Light candles, enjoy a bubble bath, or savour your morning coffee slowly. Learn to romanticise your life.

The more you enjoy your own company, the more magnetic and confident you become. You will stop craving external validation because you will already be fulfilled from within.

Letting Go of the "Relationship Equals Worth" Narrative

One of the most damaging societal beliefs is that being in a relationship somehow makes you more valuable. This is a false narrative. Your worth is not determined by your relationship status — it is inherent.

Being single does not make you unlovable, undesirable, or lacking. It makes you *whole and autonomous*. You are enough exactly as you are.

Exercise: Shifting the Singleness Mindset

Objective: Rewrite your internal narrative about being single.

- Grab a journal or piece of paper or use the worksheet at the end of the chapter.
- Write down any limiting beliefs you hold about singleness (e.g., *"I'm incomplete without a partner" or "I'll be truly happy only when I find love."*).
- Next to each belief, write a powerful and liberating affirmation that reframes it.

Example:

- Limiting Belief: *"I need someone to complete me."*
- Reframed Belief: *"I am already whole. A partner will complement me, not complete me."*

Spend a few minutes each day repeating these empowering affirmations. With time, you will begin to feel more confident and fulfilled in your singleness.

Closing Thoughts

Singleness is not a void — it is a canvas. It is your opportunity to design the life you truly desire, free from compromise. It is a time for growth, self-love, and exploration. The more you embrace it, the more empowered and magnetic you become.

You are not half of a whole — you are already whole. And when you fully embrace your wholeness, whether you meet a partner or not, you will always be complete.

WorkSheet

Chapter - 2
Embracing Solitude – Finding Comfort in Your Own Company

"You cannot be lonely if you like the person you're alone with."

– Wayne Dyer

Redefining Solitude – From Isolation to Empowerment

For many people, being alone evokes feelings of sadness, emptiness, or inadequacy. This is largely because society has conditioned us to associate solitude with loneliness. We are taught to believe that being surrounded by people or being in a relationship is the ultimate validation of our worth.

However, solitude is not the same as loneliness. *Loneliness* is a state of emotional disconnection, while *solitude* is a state of emotional self-sufficiency. When you embrace solitude, you are not running away from the world — you are running *toward yourself.*

Solitude gives you the space to reconnect with your inner world. It allows you to slow down, reflect, and deepen your self-awareness. It is in solitude that you truly meet yourself.

The Power of Enjoying Your Own Company

Think about it: you are the only person who will be with you for your entire life. Learning to enjoy your own company is not only empowering — it is essential.

When you genuinely enjoy being alone:

- You no longer depend on others for validation or entertainment.
- You develop self-trust and emotional resilience.
- You make better choices in relationships, as you are not driven by fear of being alone.
- You cultivate inner peace, which makes you more magnetic and confident.

Embracing solitude makes you realise that *you* are enough.

The Difference Between Being Alone and Feeling Lonely

It is possible to feel lonely in a crowded room and perfectly content sitting by yourself. Loneliness is not about physical isolation — it is about emotional disconnection.

When you are alone, you have the space to think, reflect, and recharge.

You feel at peace with yourself.

You are comfortable with your thoughts.

When you feel lonely, You feel emotionally unfulfilled, even in the presence of others.

You may seek external distractions to avoid facing inner discomfort.

You experience a sense of emptiness or longing for connection.

The key to transforming loneliness into fulfilling solitude is learning how to *enjoy* your own presence.

The Benefits of Embracing Solitude

Spending intentional time alone offers many benefits, including:

1. Increased Self-Awareness:

When you are alone, you have the space to reflect on your emotions, desires, and thoughts. You gain clarity on who you are, what you want, and how you feel without the influence of others.

2. Enhanced Creativity and Productivity:

Solitude provides uninterrupted time for creative thinking and focus. Many artists, writers, and innovators intentionally seek solitude to tap into their creative flow.

3. Emotional Regulation and Healing:

Being alone allows you to sit with your emotions instead of suppressing them. You learn to process feelings of sadness, grief, or anxiety healthily, building emotional resilience.

4. Freedom and Independence:

When you enjoy solitude, you no longer rely on others for your happiness. You become emotionally self-sufficient, making you more confident and independent.

Solo Activities to Enjoy Your Own Company

Embracing solitude does not mean sitting in silence all day. It is about finding meaningful ways to engage with yourself. Here are some fulfilling solo activities:

Solo Dates: Treat yourself to a coffee, dinner, or movie. Dress up and enjoy your own company without needing someone else by your side.

Creative Expression: Paint, write, sing, or dance. Use solitude as a time for creative self-expression.

Mindful Walks in Nature: Go for a walk alone. Notice the sights, sounds, and sensations around you. Let nature soothe your soul.

Solo Travel Adventures: Travelling alone may seem daunting, but it can be incredibly liberating. You learn to rely on yourself, make your own plans, and immerse yourself fully in new experiences.

Journaling and Reflection: Spend time journaling your thoughts, emotions, and dreams. Use this as a tool for self-discovery and healing.

Home Rituals: Cook a meal just for yourself, light candles, and enjoy a peaceful evening at home. Create a ritual of self-love and self-care.

Overcoming the Fear of Being Alone

If you are not used to spending time alone, it may initially feel uncomfortable. You might experience restlessness, boredom, or a desire to distract yourself with social media, TV, or calls. This is normal — it is your mind resisting stillness.

Here is how to ease into solitude:

- **Start Small:** Spend 30 minutes alone each day doing something meaningful. Gradually increase the time as you grow more comfortable.
- **Stay Off Your Phone:** Resist the urge to fill every quiet moment with digital distractions. Allow yourself too truly be present with yourself.
- **Embrace the Discomfort:** If feelings of loneliness arise, sit with them instead of running from them. Allow yourself to feel and process them.

The more you practice solitude, the more you will find comfort and peace in your own presence.

Exercise: The Solo Challenge

Objective: Develop comfort with solitude by intentionally spending time alone.

Instructions:

1. Choose one day within the next week to dedicate entirely to yourself.
2. Plan three solo activities that bring you joy or relaxation. Examples include:
    - A nature walks or hike.
    - A solo lunch or dinner at a restaurant.
    - A creative activity (painting, writing, or baking).
3. Turn off social media and minimize external distractions during this time.
4. Reflect on how you feel during and after the experience.

Journal Prompt:

After completing the challenge, reflect on the following:

- How did it feel to spend intentional time alone?
- What did you discover about yourself?
- Did you feel more /or less connected to yourself?

Repeat this solo challenge regularly to strengthen your connection with yourself and find comfort in your own company.

Closing Thoughts

Embracing solitude is one of the greatest gifts you can give yourself. When you learn to enjoy your own company, you become emotionally self-sufficient. You stop seeking external validation and start cultivating internal fulfilment.

Remember:

- Solitude is not a void — it is an opportunity for self-connection.
- You are never truly alone when you are at peace with yourself.
- The deeper you connect with yourself, the richer your life becomes.

So, take yourself out on a date. Treat yourself with kindness. Enjoy the pleasure of your own company. Be your own best companion.

Worksheet

Chapter - 3
The Art of Self-Love – Becoming Your Own Best Friend

"To love oneself is the beginning of a lifelong romance."

– Oscar Wilde

Why Self-Love Is the Key to Being Happy Alone

At the heart of being alone without feeling lonely is self-love. It is the foundation upon which your happiness, emotional stability, and inner peace rest. When you cultivate genuine self-love, you no longer rely on others for validation, affection, or fulfilment. Instead, you become your own source of love, acceptance, and joy.

However, self-love is more than just spa days or self-care rituals — it is about developing a deep, compassionate, and nurturing relationship with yourself. It means accepting yourself fully — flaws and all — and becoming your own greatest ally and best friend.

Remember:

- Self-love is the foundation of emotional independence.
- It empowers you to enjoy your own company and feel complete without external validation.
- Healing the relationship with yourself is essential for self-acceptance and emotional well-being.
- With self-love, solitude becomes a source of peace, not loneliness.

What Is Self-Love, and Why Is It Essential?

Many people confuse self-love with arrogance or self-indulgence. Actually, Self-love is the act of treating yourself with the same kindness, care, and compassion you would offer a loved one. It means prioritising your emotional well-being and respecting your needs.

Self-Love Is:

- Practising self-compassion during difficult times.
- Accepting your imperfections without self-criticism.
- Prioritising your well-being and emotional health.

- Setting healthy boundaries and protecting your peace.
- Speaking to yourself with kindness and encouragement.

Why Is Self-Love Essential?

- **Prevents Loneliness:** When you enjoy your own company, you no longer feel alone.
- **Increases Self-Worth:** You stop seeking validation from others.
- **Improves Relationships:** You attract healthier, more fulfilling connections.
- **Reduces Emotional Dependency:** You no longer rely on others to fill emotional voids.

Reflection Exercise:

- Write down three ways you already practice self-love (e.g., prioritising rest, celebrating your achievements).
- List three areas where you want to deepen your self-love (e.g., being kinder to yourself, prioritising self-care).

Recognising Signs of Low Self-Love

Before you can fully nurture self-love, it is important to identify areas where you may be lacking it. Here are common signs that you may need to deepen your self-love:

- **Self-Criticism:** Constantly putting yourself down or doubting your worth.

- **Neglecting Your Needs:** Prioritising others at the expense of your own well-being.
- **Seeking Validation:** Relying on external approval to feel worthy.
- **Fear of Being Alone:** Feeling incomplete or unworthy without a partner.
- **Negative Self-Talk:** Engaging in harsh inner dialogue.

Reflection Exercise:

- Take a moment to reflect:
  - Do you often harshly criticise yourself?
  - Are you uncomfortable being alone?
  - Do you sacrifice your needs for others?
- Write down any patterns or behaviours that indicate areas where your self-love could be strengthened.

Healing the Relationship with Yourself

To truly embrace self-love, you need to heal the relationship you have with yourself. This involves practising self-compassion, releasing self-limiting beliefs, and treating yourself with the same kindness you would offer a loved one.

a) Practising Self-Compassion:

- Be gentle with yourself when you make mistakes.
- Offer yourself the same forgiveness and empathy you would give to a close friend.
- Release self-judgment and practice gentle self-forgiveness.

Exercise:

- The next time you catch yourself being self-critical, pause.
- Ask yourself:
  - "Would I say this to someone I love?"
- If not, reframe your inner dialogue with compassion.
- Example:
  - Instead of: "I'm such a failure," say: "I am learning and growing, and that is enough."

b) Releasing Self-Limiting Beliefs:

Lack of self-love often stems from negative beliefs about yourself. These beliefs hold you back from experiencing self-worth.

- Identify disempowering beliefs such as:
  - "I'm not good enough" or "I am unlovable."
- Replace them with empowering affirmations.

Exercise:

- Write down 3 self-limiting beliefs you hold.
- Rewrite them as positive affirmations.
- Example:
    - "I am incomplete without a partner" → "I am whole and complete on my own."
    - "I am not worthy of love" → "I am inherently worthy of love and respect."

Developing a Daily Self-Love Practice

Like any relationship, your relationship with yourself requires regular nurturing. By creating consistent self-love rituals, you reinforce feelings of worthiness and self-acceptance.

a) Mirror Work:

Stand in front of a mirror, make eye contact with yourself, and say loving affirmations aloud.

- "I am worthy."
- "I am beautiful, inside and out."
- "I love and accept myself fully."

Exercise:

- Commit to 5 minutes of mirror work every morning.
- Notice how your relationship with yourself deepens over time.

b) Self-Care Rituals:

Engage in activities that nourish your body, mind, and soul.

- Solo Dates: Take yourself out for dinner, visit a museum, or go for a scenic walk.
- Relaxing Rituals: Create a soothing evening routine with candles, music, and self-care.
- Creative Expression: Engage in art, writing, or dance to express yourself.

Exercise:

- Schedule a weekly "self-date" where you treat yourself with the same love and attention you would offer a partner or friend.

Embracing Your Flaws and Imperfections

True self-love means embracing your imperfections rather than striving for perfection. It is about accepting yourself fully — flaws, quirks, and all.

a) Releasing the Need for Perfection:

- Let go of unrealistic expectations.
- Accept that you are human — and perfectly imperfect.

b) Celebrating Your Uniqueness:

- Your quirks and flaws make you authentic and beautiful.
- Embrace your individuality instead of comparing yourself to others.

Exercise:

- Write a letter to yourself, celebrating your flaws and unique traits.
- Example:
  - "Dear [Your Name], I love your quirky sense of humour and your compassionate heart. I embrace your clumsiness and your spontaneous spirit — it makes you uniquely you. You are worthy of love, just as you are."

Falling in Love with Your Own Company

The ultimate expression of self-love is genuinely enjoying your own company. When you reach this stage, solitude becomes a source of joy, not loneliness.

Ways to Enjoy Your Own Company:

- **Solo Adventures:** Travel alone, take yourself on a solo date, or explore new hobbies.
- **Enjoy Being in Your Own Space:** Create a cosy environment that feels nurturing and inspiring.
- **Celebrate Your Independence:** Relish the freedom and autonomy of being single.

Exercise:

- Plan a full "me day" dedicated entirely to yourself.
- Do things that bring you joy — whether it is exploring a new place, indulging in a creative hobby, or simply relaxing at home.

Conclusion: You Are Your Own Greatest Love Story

The relationship you have with yourself sets the tone for every other relationship in your life. When you master self-love, you no longer seek external validation — you become whole and complete on your own.

Final Thought:

"Fall in love with taking care of yourself — mind, body, and soul. You are your own greatest love story."

Worksheet

Chapter - 4
Cultivating Self-Confidence – Boosting Your Self-Esteem as A Single Individual

"Your value does not decrease based on your relationship status. You are whole, worthy, and enough — just as you are."

The Power of Self-Confidence in Singlehood

Confidence is one of the most attractive and empowering qualities a person can have, whether they are single or in a relationship. However, when you are single, it can sometimes feel like your confidence takes a hit — especially if you have internalised the belief that your worth is tied to being coupled.

Society often glorifies romantic relationships, making singleness feel like a flaw rather than a season of growth and self-discovery. However, the truth is:

- Your self-worth is not defined by your relationship status.
- You are inherently valuable, complete, and enough — on your own.
- Your confidence can thrive and flourish while single, making you emotionally independent and self-assured.

In this chapter, you will learn:

- The root causes of low self-confidence when single.
- How to shift your mindset and embrace self-assurance.
- Practical strategies to build self-esteem and self-worth.
- How to radiate confidence in your daily life.
- The link between confidence and emotional independence.

1. Understanding the Link Between Singleness and Confidence

It is easy to tie self-worth to external factors — relationship status, validation from others, or social approval. When you are single, you might occasionally feel "less than" because you are not part of a couple. This false belief can chip away at your self-confidence.

Common Confidence Struggles When Single:

- **Feeling "not chosen":** You may sometimes interpret being single as a sign that you are not desirable or lovable — but your value has nothing to do with whether someone chooses you.
- **Comparison to others:** Seeing friends, colleagues, or family members in relationships can make you feel like you are "falling behind" or missing out.
- **Negative self-talk:** Thoughts like "I'm not good enough" or "No one will want me" can diminish your self-esteem.
- **Fear of being judged:** You might worry that others view you as flawed or unworthy because you are single.
- **Validation-seeking behaviours:** Seeking constant reassurance through dating apps or social media likes can make your confidence dependent on external validation.

Reflection Exercise: Ask yourself:

- Do you tie your confidence to your relationship status?
- Are you overly critical of yourself because you are single?
- Do you compare yourself to people in relationships?
- Do you engage in validation-seeking behaviours like frequent swiping, social media posting or settling for less in relationships for a confidence boost? Write down your answers and identify any patterns of external validation-seeking.

2. Shifting Your Mindset – You Are Enough

The first step to cultivating unshakable self-confidence as a single individual is rewriting the narrative. Being single is not a flaw or a failure — it is a season of self-empowerment, growth, and freedom.

Mindset Shifts for Self-Confidence:

- From "I'm incomplete" to "I am whole and fulfilled."
- From "I'm not wanted" to "I am valuable and worthy on my own."
- From "I need someone to complete me" to "I am already complete."
- From "I'll be happy when I meet someone" to "I create my own happiness now."

- From "I am missing out" to "I am gaining self-mastery and independence."

Affirmations for Confidence: Speak these affirmations daily:

- *"I am whole and complete on my own."*
- *"I am valuable and worthy, regardless of my relationship status."*
- *"I radiate confidence, strength, and self-assurance."*
- *"I love and accept myself fully."*
- *"My happiness comes from within."*

Exercise:

Write down five limiting beliefs you have about yourself as a single person (e.g., "I cannot do……. without a partner").

- Next, rewrite each limiting belief into a positive affirmation (e.g., "I am capable of doing anything I want").
- Repeat these affirmations daily to rewire your mindset.

3. Building Genuine Self-Confidence

Confidence is not about being perfect — it is about accepting yourself fully and showing up authentically. The key to cultivating self-confidence while single is to root it in self-acceptance, self-compassion, and self-respect.

Practical Ways to Build Self-Confidence:

a) Embrace Your Strengths and Talents

- **Identify your unique strengths:** Are you creative, empathetic, resourceful, or witty?
- **Celebrate your talents:** Write a list of skills, qualities, and accomplishments that make you proud.
- **Showcase your talents:** Share your skills through creative projects, hobbies, or volunteering.

Exercise:

Write down 10 things you love about yourself — your character, values, and strengths. Revisit this list whenever you feel self-doubt.

b) Boost Your Self-Image

Your external presentation can influence your internal confidence. When you feel good about how you look, you carry yourself with greater self-assurance.

- **Invest in self-care:** Prioritise grooming, skincare, and physical wellness.
- **Dress in ways that empower you:** Choose outfits that make you feel confident and stylish, even if you are dressing for yourself.
- **Adopt confident body language:** Stand tall, make eye contact, and own your space.

Exercise:

Plan a "confidence-boosting day" where you:

- Dress in an outfit that makes you feel attractive and radiant.
- Walk with a strong and confident posture.
- Make deliberate eye contact and smile at strangers. Notice how your physical presentation affects your inner confidence.

c) Set and Achieve Small Goals

Self-confidence grows when you prove to yourself that you are capable.

- **Set micro-goals:** small wins (e.g., learning a new recipe, speaking up in a meeting, or going on a solo adventure) boost your self-esteem.
- **Celebrate your achievements:** No matter how small, acknowledge and reward yourself for your progress.
- **Challenge your comfort zone:** Try activities that push you out of your routine (public speaking, dancing, or trying a new sport).

Exercise:

Write down three goals you want to achieve in the next month.

- Break them into small, actionable steps.
- Celebrate each milestone as you complete it.

4. Self-Love and Self-Compassion

Confidence is deeply rooted in self-love and self-acceptance. When you treat yourself with kindness, your self-esteem naturally flourishes.

Ways to Cultivate Self-Love:

- **Practice self-care rituals:** Take yourself out for solo dates, enjoy a spa day, or engage in activities that bring you joy.
- **Speak kindly to yourself:** Replace self-criticism with compassionate self-talk.
- **Prioritise your needs:** Set healthy boundaries and prioritise your emotional well-being.
- **Celebrate yourself:** Do not wait for a partner to buy you flowers — buy them yourself and treat yourself to small gifts and celebrations.

Exercise:

Write a love letter to yourself, highlighting your strengths, accomplishments, and the things you admire about yourself. Read it whenever you feel your confidence wavering.

5. Radiating Confidence in Daily Life

Once you have cultivated inner confidence, let it shine in your daily life.

- **Speak with conviction:** Use a confident tone and clear speech.

- **Own your space:** Walk with a strong posture and own your physical presence.
- **Engage authentically:** Make eye contact, smile warmly, and exude genuine warmth.
- **Stop seeking external validation:** Trust your own self-worth instead of relying on approval from others.

Exercise:

- For the next week, practice one confident behaviour daily.
- It could be initiating a conversation, maintaining a strong posture, or expressing your opinion boldly.
- Notice how it makes you feel.

Closing Thoughts: Confidence is Your Superpower

Being single is not a sign of lack — it is a season of self-mastery and confidence-building. When you cultivate genuine self-esteem, you no longer seek validation through relationships — you radiate confidence from within.

Final Reminders:

- You are enough, just as you are.
- Confidence comes from self-acceptance, not external validation.

- Your worth is not defined by your relationship status.

Own your singleness with confidence, authenticity, and pride — you are whole and complete, exactly as you are.

Worksheet

Chapter - 5

Overcoming Loneliness Triggers – Recognizing and Navigating Moments of Emotional Vulnerability

"Loneliness is not the absence of people — it is the absence of connection. The most important connection you can cultivate is the one with yourself."

Understanding Loneliness Triggers

Being single does not automatically mean you will feel lonely. In fact, many people in relationships also experience loneliness. Loneliness is not about being physically alone — it is about feeling emotionally disconnected, misunderstood, or lacking meaningful connection.

Even when you are building a fulfilling solo life, moments of emotional vulnerability can still surface. Certain triggers — like special occasions, social media, or seeing happy couples — can activate feelings of loneliness. It is important to recognise these triggers, understand the emotions they bring up, and develop healthy ways to navigate them.

In this chapter, you will learn:

- How to identify common loneliness triggers.
- Strategies for processing emotional vulnerability.
- Tools to reframe and redirect feelings of loneliness.
- How to cultivate emotional resilience and self-connection.

1. Recognising Common Loneliness Triggers

Loneliness often sneaks up on you when you least expect it. Being aware of what triggers these feelings helps you respond intentionally rather than react impulsively.

Common Loneliness Triggers:

- **Social Media Comparison:** Seeing highlight reels of happy couples or families can make you feel like you are missing out, even when you are content with your life.

- **Holidays and Special Occasions:** Birthdays, Valentine's Day, weddings, or family events can intensify feelings of being "left out" or alone.
- **Idle Time or Boredom:** When you have unstructured time, loneliness can creep in, making you feel restless or aimless.
- **Memories of Past Relationships:** Running into an ex, visiting familiar places, or certain dates can stir up feelings of nostalgia or sadness.
- **Emotional Fatigue:** Long, stressful days or periods of emotional exhaustion can make you more vulnerable to loneliness.
- **Romantic Media:** Movies, books, or shows centred around love stories can evoke longing, especially during moments of emotional sensitivity.
- **Moments of Accomplishment:** Ironically, achieving goals without someone to share them with can sometimes leave you feeling lonely.

Reflection Exercise:

Write down your personal loneliness triggers. Ask yourself:

- When do I most often feel lonely?
- What situations or experiences intensify this feeling?
- Are there certain times of day or year when I am more vulnerable?

2. The Emotional Impact of Loneliness

When loneliness is triggered, it can activate a range of emotional responses. The key is to recognise these emotions without judgment and learn how to process them healthily.

Common Emotional Responses to Loneliness:

- **Sadness:** You may feel disheartened, nostalgic, or mournful for what you feel is missing.
- **Self-Criticism:** Loneliness can sometimes trigger negative self-talk, making you question your worth or feel "unlovable." You may blame yourself for the breakup.
- **Restlessness or Anxiety:** The discomfort of loneliness can make you seek external distractions (e.g., social media scrolling or impulsive social plans) as a coping mechanism.
- **Longing for Connection:** You may feel a deep yearning for companionship, intimacy, or closeness with others.
- **Numbness or Apathy:** Chronic loneliness can sometimes lead to emotional detachment or a sense of disconnection.

Exercise: Identifying Your Emotional Responses. The next time you feel lonely, take a moment to pause and reflect:

- What specific emotion am I feeling? (Sadness, longing, frustration, etc.)

- Where do I feel this emotion in my body? (Tightness in the chest, heaviness in the shoulders, etc.)
- What thought or belief is associated with this emotion? (E.g., “I am missing out” or “I am not enough”)

3. Healthy Ways to Navigate Loneliness

When loneliness strikes, it is important to have healthy coping mechanisms in place. Rather than numbing or avoiding the feeling, you can use the moment as an opportunity for self-connection, self-compassion, and self-discovery.

a) Create a Self-Soothing Ritual

Loneliness often triggers a need for comfort and emotional regulation. Creating a soothing self-care ritual helps you nurture yourself during moments of vulnerability.

Self-Soothing Ideas:

- **Sensory Comfort:** Wrap yourself in a cosy blanket, light a scented candle, or take a warm bath.
- **Calming Music or Sounds:** Listen to peaceful instrumental music or nature sounds.
- **Comforting Scents:** Use essential oils like lavender or chamomile to promote relaxation.
- **Grounding Techniques:** Walk barefoot on grass or hug a tree or hold a comforting object (a soft pillow, stuffed animal) to feel grounded.

Pro Tip: Create a "loneliness comfort box" filled with small items that bring you peace — like a handwritten letter to yourself, a meaningful photo, or a soothing playlist.

b) Practice Emotional Validation

Rather than suppressing feelings of loneliness, allow yourself to acknowledge and validate them. Emotions become less overwhelming when you give permit yourself to feel them.

Steps for Emotional Validation:

1. **Pause and Breathe:** When you feel a wave of loneliness, pause and take three slow, deep breaths.

2. **Acknowledge the Emotion:** Silently say, "I am feeling lonely at this time, and that is okay. It is a valid human emotion."

3. **Validate Yourself:** Remind yourself that feeling lonely does not mean you are broken or lacking. It simply means you are human.

Mantra for Validation: "I am allowed to feel lonely sometimes. It does not define me. I am whole and complete as I am."

c) Redirect Your Energy with Purposeful Action

Loneliness tends to create a void of inactivity or passivity. Redirecting your focus to purposeful, creative, or active experiences can help you shift your emotional state.

Purposeful Activities to Combat Loneliness:

- **Get Creative:** Write, paint, cook, or start a creative project that immerses you in self-expression.
- **Move Your Body:** Go for a walk, dance, or practice yoga to release emotional tension.
- **Volunteer or Help Someone:** Acts of service can create a sense of connection and reduce feelings of isolation.
- **Learn Something New:** Watch a documentary, take an online class, or explore a new hobby to engage your mind.

d) Connect with Your Support Network

While being single offers independence, it does not mean you have to go through loneliness alone. Reach out to your support network — whether friends, family, or like-minded groups — to cultivate meaningful human connections.

Ways to Reach Out:

- **Call or Video Chat:** Hearing a familiar voice can instantly reduce feelings of isolation.
- **Join a Group Activity:** Attend a class, workshop, or hobby group where you can meet new people.
- **Express Vulnerability:** Let a trusted friend know how you are feeling. Sometimes, simply being heard can ease loneliness.

4. Transforming Loneliness into Solitude

There is a profound difference between loneliness and solitude.

- Loneliness is the discomfort of being disconnected.
- Solitude is the peaceful enjoyment of being with yourself.

By consciously practising solitude, you can transform lonely moments into opportunities for self-nourishment and reflection.

Ways to Cultivate Peaceful Solitude:

- **Create a Mindful Ritual:** Enjoy your morning coffee or tea slowly, without distractions.
- **Spend Time in Nature:** Go for a solo walk in the park or sit by the water.
- **Write or Journal:** Use solitude as an opportunity for self-reflection and creative expression.
- **Practice Mindfulness:** Meditate or engage in breathing exercises to cultivate inner stillness.

5. Building Emotional Resilience

Overcoming loneliness is not about avoiding it — it is about building the emotional resilience to navigate it with strength and self-compassion.

Resilience-Building Practices:

- **Daily Gratitude:** Keep a gratitude journal to focus on what you have, rather than what you lack.

- **Mindful Self-Compassion:** Practice self-kindness during vulnerable moments.
- **Challenge Negative Thoughts:** When loneliness triggers self-critical thoughts, reframe them with kindness.
- **Affirm Your Worth:** Remind yourself that your value is not defined by your relationship status.

Closing Thoughts: You Are Never Truly Alone

Loneliness is a temporary emotional state — not a permanent reality. When you learn to navigate loneliness with self-compassion and emotional awareness, you become stronger, more self-connected, and more resilient.

Final Reminder:

- You are whole — even when you feel lonely.
- You are worthy — whether you are with someone or alone.
- Your own company is valuable — cherish it.

Embrace the beauty of your solo journey. You are never truly alone — you always have yourself.

Worksheet

Chapter - 6

Rediscovering Yourself – Embracing Self-Growth & Personal Development

"The most powerful relationship you will ever have is the one you have with yourself."

– Diane Von Furstenberg

The Beauty of Self-Rediscovery

Being single is not a state of lack — it is an invitation for self-discovery. When you are on your own, you have the rare freedom to focus entirely on yourself — your passions, growth, and evolution — without the compromises and distractions of a relationship. It is a beautiful opportunity to rediscover who you truly are, beyond societal labels or the influence of others.

Many people lose parts of themselves in relationships — sacrificing their personal dreams, interests, or authenticity. Being single offers you the chance to reclaim those lost parts, uncover new dimensions of yourself, and grow into the most empowered, authentic, and self-assured version of you.

You need to learn how to:

- Reconnect with your authentic self through self-reflection.
- Cultivate a growth mindset and embrace lifelong learning.
- Explore new passions, skills, and hobbies.
- Foster emotional growth and resilience.
- Create a personal development plan for ongoing self-expansion.

1. The Journey of Rediscovery – Who Are You Without a Partner?

When you are in a relationship, it is easy to unknowingly merge your identity with your partner's. You may compromise on preferences, hobbies, or goals to create harmony. Once you are single, you have the freedom to reclaim your individuality and discover the person you are outside of a partnership.

Reflection Exercise: Unveiling Your Authentic Self

To rediscover yourself, reflect on the following questions:

- Who were you before your last relationship?
    - What hobbies, passions, or goals did you put aside?
- What makes you feel alive?
    - When do you feel most authentic and joyful?
- What would you do if no one's opinion mattered?
    - How would you dress, behave, or express yourself?
- What new parts of yourself do you want to explore?
    - Skills, talents, or interests you have always been curious about.

Exercise:

- Write down three forgotten or unexplored passions you want to reconnect with.
- Commit to incorporating them into your weekly routine.

2. Cultivating a Growth Mindset – Evolving Through Self-Expansion

Rediscovering yourself requires openness to growth. A growth mindset means believing that you are capable of learning, evolving, and transforming. It is about being excited to try new things, learn from mistakes, and embrace personal expansion.

Signs You Are Cultivating a Growth Mindset:

You view challenges as opportunities to learn and improve.

Your welcome feedback and use it constructively.

You embrace new experiences without fear of failure.

You recognise that personal development is a lifelong journey.

You celebrate progress over perfection.

Ways to Embrace a Growth Mindset:

- **Try new things regularly:** Step out of your comfort zone by exploring unfamiliar activities.
- **Reframe mistakes as lessons:** Do not fear failure — it's a stepping stone to growth.
- **Adopt a curious mindset:** Stay open-minded and curious about new skills, people, and ideas.
- **Celebrate self-improvement:** Track and celebrate small personal victories.

Exercise:

- Write down one skill or activity you have always wanted to learn.
- Research a course or workshop and sign up for it this week.

3. Discovering New Passions and Hobbies

Being single gives you the freedom to explore passions without compromise. You can rediscover old hobbies or dive into entirely new ones that excite you.

Why Exploring New Interests Matters:

- **It strengthens your identity:** Hobbies shape who you are and what you value.
- **It boosts creativity and joy:** Engaging in new activities sparks inspiration.
- **It creates a fulfilling life:** You become less dependent on external validation for happiness.

How to Explore New Passions:

Creative Exploration:

- Try painting, photography, music, or writing.
- Take a pottery or dance class.
- Start a blog or YouTube channel about a personal interest.

Physical Adventures:

- Experiment with different forms of movement or fitness.
- Try hiking, boxing, rock climbing, or Pilates.
- Join group fitness classes for a social boost.

Travel and Exploration:

- Plan solo trips or weekend getaways.
- Explore nearby towns or hidden gems in your city.
- Be spontaneous — visit a new café or museum.

Exercise:

- Make a list of 5 new hobbies or activities you want to try.
- Commit to exploring one new activity per month.

4. Emotional Growth and Self-Awareness

Rediscovering yourself also involves emotional growth and inner reflection. As you spend more time alone, you have the chance to:

- Deepen your self-awareness.
- Heal emotional wounds from past relationships.
- Strengthen your emotional resilience.

Practices for Emotional Growth:

Mindfulness and Meditation:

- Practice mindfulness to observe your emotions without judgment.
- Use meditation to develop emotional balance.

Journaling for Self-Discovery:

- Write about your feelings, experiences, and aspirations.
- Use journal prompts to explore your emotions:
  - *"What parts of myself do I want to nurture?"*
  - *"What does happiness look like to me now?"*
  - *"How can I honour my emotional needs?"*

Therapy or Coaching:

- Work with a therapist or life coach to deepen your self-awareness.
- Seek support for emotional healing or personal growth.

Exercise:

- Start a self-reflection journal and write in its weekly.
- Set a goal to explore one emotional growth practice (like meditation or therapy) each month.

5. Building Self-Confidence Through Growth

As you invest in self-growth, your confidence naturally strengthens. The more you develop skills, learn new things, and explore passions, the more you realise your capabilities and worth.

Ways to Build Self-Confidence:

- **Celebrate small wins:** Acknowledge every step of progress, no matter how small.
- **Push your comfort zone:** Challenge yourself by doing things that scare you.
- **Learn self-reliance:** Become comfortable with solo adventures, meals, and activities.
- **Prioritise self-compassion:** Be kind to yourself when you face setbacks.
- **Embrace authenticity:** Stop seeking external validation and express your true self.

Exercise:

- Identify one area where you feel insecure or lack confidence.
- Create an action plan to gradually improve it (e.g., public speaking, fitness, or creativity).
- Track your progress weekly.

6. Creating a Personal Development Plan

To stay committed to self-growth, create a personal development plan. This is a roadmap for how you want to evolve in different areas of your life.

How to Create Your Personal Growth Plan:

1. **Identify Key Areas of Growth:**
    - **Emotional growth:** (e.g., therapy, self-awareness)
    - **Skills and knowledge:** (e.g., learning new subjects or skills)
    - **Physical health:** (e.g., fitness, wellness practices)
    - **Creative expression:** (e.g., hobbies, artistic projects)
2. **Set Clear Goals:**
    - Choose 2-3 growth goals for each area.
    - **Example:**
        - **Emotional:** Practice daily mindfulness.
        - **Physical:** Join a yoga class twice a week.

- **Learning:** Read one personal development book monthly.

3. **Track Your Progress:**
    - Use a journal or app to track milestones and reflect on your growth journey.

Exercise:

- Create your personal development plan with specific goals and a timeline.
- Schedule regular check-ins to review your progress.

Closing Thoughts: Becoming Your Best Self

Rediscovering yourself is not about changing who you are — it is about becoming more of who you have always been. When you embrace self-growth, you step into your power, authenticity, and confidence.

Remember:

- You are a work in progress and a masterpiece at the same time.
- You deserve to evolve, expand, and rediscover your greatness.
- This solo season is your time to blossom into the most radiant version of you.

Worksheet

Chapter - 7

Mindfulness & Mental Health – Tools to Find Peace and Happiness Within Yourself

"Be where you are; otherwise, you will miss your life."

– Jim Elliot

The Power of Mindfulness for Singles

In the hustle of daily life, it is easy to become disconnected from yourself. As a single person, moments of solitude can sometimes lead to overthinking, self-criticism, or feelings of emptiness. However, the key to inner peace and happiness does not lie in external circumstances — it resides within you. The practice of mindfulness offers you the ability to cultivate a calm, clear, and joyful state of being, no matter what your relationship status is.

Mindfulness is more than just a practice — it is a way of life. It teaches you to become fully present in the moment, release mental chatter, and embrace stillness. Through regular mindfulness practices, you can reduce stress, manage anxiety, enhance self-awareness, and discover true happiness within yourself.

How mindfulness will help you:

- Mindfulness anchors you in the present moment, preventing overthinking and worry.
- As a single person, mindfulness enhances emotional stability and self-compassion.
- Regular practice strengthens your mental health and resilience.
- True happiness comes from inner peace, not external validation.

What is Mindfulness?

Mindfulness is the practice of being fully present and aware of your thoughts, feelings, and surroundings without judgment. It involves consciously observing your experiences as they unfold, rather than getting lost in thoughts or emotional reactions.

Core Principles of Mindfulness:

- **Present-Moment Awareness:** Focusing on the here and now rather than dwelling on the past or worrying about the future.

- **Non-Judgmental Observation:** Not labelling experiences as good or bad — simply observing them as they are.
- **Acceptance:** Embracing your emotions and thoughts with compassion rather than resistance.
- **Breath Awareness:** Using the breath as an anchor to the present moment.

How Mindfulness Will Benefit you as a Single person:

- **Reduces Loneliness:** By being present with yourself, you feel less disconnected.
- **Improves Emotional Regulation:** Mindfulness helps you observe emotions without being consumed by them.
- **Enhances Self-Love:** It fosters self-compassion and self-acceptance.
- **Increases Joy in Solitude:** You learn to enjoy your own company without seeking external distractions.

Reflection Exercise:

- Sit in a quiet place and close your eyes.
- Take a few deep breaths and slowly observe your surroundings using your senses.
- What do you hear, smell, and feel?
- Simply observe without judgment.

- Notice how this simple practice creates a sense of calm and presence.

Mindfulness for Mental Health – Reducing Stress & Anxiety

As a single person, you may sometimes feel overwhelmed by thoughts of the future, societal pressures, or self-doubt. Mindfulness offers you the tools to soothe your mind and regulate your emotions.

How Mindfulness Supports Mental Health:

- **Reduces Anxiety:** Mindfulness shifts your focus from anxious thoughts to the present moment, calming the nervous system.
- **Lowers Stress:** Breathing exercises and body scans release physical tension and emotional stress.
- **Increases Self-Awareness:** By observing your thought patterns, you become more aware of negative self-talk and can consciously shift it.
- **Improves Emotional Stability:** Regular practice strengthens your ability to remain calm in emotionally charged situations.

Simple Mindfulness Techniques to Reduce Stress:

1. **Breath Awareness:** Close your eyes and take slow, deep breaths. With each inhale, feel your belly expand. With each exhale, feel it contract. Focus on the sensation of the breath moving in and out.

2. **Grounding Technique:** Engage your senses. Name:
    - 5 things you can see
    - 4 things you can touch
    - 3 things you can hear
    - 2 things you can smell
    - 1 thing you can taste.

This practice grounds you in the present and calms your mind.

Exercise:

- The next time you feel stressed or anxious, pause and practice 5 minutes of mindful breathing.
- Inhale deeply for a count of 4, hold for 5, and exhale slowly for 6.
- Notice how your body and mind gradually relax.

Cultivating Self-Compassion Through Mindfulness

One of the most powerful gifts of mindfulness is self-compassion — the ability to treat yourself with kindness, especially during moments of struggle. As a single person, practising self-compassion ensures that you become your own source of comfort and validation.

What is Self-Compassion?

- **Self-Kindness:** Speaking to yourself with kindness rather than self-criticism.

- **Common Humanity:** Recognising that everyone experiences challenges — you are not alone.
- **Mindful Acceptance:** Allowing yourself to feel emotions without self-judgment.

Mindful Self-Compassion Practices:

- **Loving-Kindness Meditation:** Sit comfortably and close your eyes. Inhale deeply and exhale slowly. Silently repeat the following affirmations:
    - "May I be kind to myself."
    - "May I be at peace."
    - "May I love and accept myself as I am."
- **Self-Soothing Touch:** When you feel overwhelmed, place your hand over your heart or gently hug yourself. This simple gesture activates your body's self-soothing response.
- **Reframing Negative Self-Talk:** Each time you catch yourself in self-criticism, pause. Ask yourself, "How would I speak to a dear friend in this situation?" Use the same gentle tone with yourself.

Exercise:

- For one week, practice a self-compassion affirmation daily.
- Each morning, place your hand over your heart and say, "I am worthy. I am enough. I am loved."

- Notice how this shifts your inner dialogue over time.

Mindful Gratitude – Cultivating Joy from Within

Gratitude is a powerful mindfulness practice that shifts your focus from what you lack to what you have. As a single person, practising gratitude brings you back to the beauty of your present life, enhancing contentment and happiness.

How Gratitude Benefits Mental Health:

- **Boosts Positivity:** Gratitude rewires your brain to focus on positive experiences.
- **Reduces Stress:** It lowers cortisol levels, reducing stress.
- **Increases Resilience:** Grateful individuals are more emotionally resilient.
- **Improves Sleep:** Gratitude practices promote relaxation and improve sleep quality.

Mindful Gratitude Practices:

1. **Gratitude Journaling:** Each night, write down three things you are grateful for. Be specific. Instead of "I'm grateful for my friends," write "I'm grateful for the heartfelt conversation I had with my friend today."
2. **Gratitude Walk:** During a nature walk, focus on the beauty around you — the colours, the sounds, the scents. Silently express gratitude for each detail.

3. **Gratitude Meditation:** Sit comfortably. Close your eyes. With each inhale, visualise receiving love and gratitude. With each exhale, send gratitude out into the world. When I do grounding, I have made it a practice to thank Mother Earth for grounding my energies and the grass for cushioning my feet.

Exercise:

- For the next seven days, practice gratitude journaling every evening.
- Write down three things you are grateful for, no matter how small.
- Notice how it shifts your mindset and emotional well-being.

Creating a Daily Mindfulness Routine for Singles

Consistency is the key to reaping the benefits of mindfulness. By creating a daily routine, you establish a sustainable practice that nourishes your mind, body, and soul.

Sample Daily Mindfulness Routine:

- **Morning:** 5-10 minutes of breath awareness meditation.
- **Midday:** A mindful and aware nature walk or gratitude break.
- **Evening:** 10 minutes of body scan relaxation or loving-kindness meditation.
- **Night:** Gratitude journaling before sleep.

Exercise:

- Design your personalised daily mindfulness routine.
- Choose at least one practice for morning, afternoon, and evening.
- Commit to practising consistently for two weeks.

Mindfulness as Your Path to Inner Peace

As a single person, cultivating mindfulness allows you to embrace the beauty of solitude with grace and joy. It strengthens your mental health, enhances self-awareness, and connects you to the present moment. Through mindfulness, you discover that happiness and fulfilment are not dependent on external circumstances — they reside within you.

"True happiness is not found in another person — it is discovered within yourself. Through mindfulness, you unlock the boundless peace and joy that have always been yours."

Worksheet

Chapter - 8
Building A Fulfilling Solo Life – Cultivating Purpose and Joy Alone

"You do not need another person to complete you. You only need to realise you are already whole."

Shifting the Mindset – Alone Does Not Mean Empty

One of the greatest misconceptions about being single is that life somehow lacks fulfilment or meaning without a partner. This belief often causes people to chase relationships in an attempt to fill an internal void.

However, true fulfilment does not come from external connections — it comes from *within.*

Building a fulfilling solo life means creating a life that is so rich, meaningful, and joyful that you do not feel the need to be with someone just to feel whole. You no longer look at your life as something that is "on hold" until the right person comes along. Instead, you live fully and intentionally in the present.

A fulfilling solo life is not just about staying busy — it is about *living with purpose*. It means discovering passions, nurturing personal growth, and filling your days with activities and experiences that light you up.

The Power of Purpose When You Are Single

When you cultivate a sense of purpose, you become self-sufficient. You no longer rely on relationships for happiness or validation. Your purpose becomes the driving force behind your joy, guiding you through life with enthusiasm and passion.

Why Purpose Matters:

- It gives your life meaning, regardless of your relationship status.
- It helps you feel motivated, inspired, and fulfilled.
- It strengthens your sense of identity and self-worth.
- It makes you more attractive to others by making you confident and self-assured.

Your purpose does not have to be grand or world-changing — it simply needs to *matter to you*. It could be your career, a creative passion, volunteering, spiritual growth, or even the simple joy of lifelong learning.

Finding Your Solo Passion

When you are single, you have a golden opportunity to explore your passions and discover what makes you feel alive. Use this time to reconnect with hobbies, dreams, and interests you may have set aside.

Questions to help you discover your passions:

- What activities make you lose track of time?
- What did you enjoy doing as a child?
- What subjects or skills have you always wanted to learn?
- What creative outlets bring you joy?
- When do you feel most alive?

Examples of Solo Passions:

- **Creative Outlets:** Painting, writing, cooking, photography, or crafting.
- **Physical Activities:** Dancing, yoga, hiking, or weight training.
- **Learning & Growth:** Taking courses, reading, or exploring new fields of knowledge.
- **Service-Oriented Passions:** Volunteering, mentoring, or helping others.

- **Travel and Exploration:** Solo trips, discovering new places, or cultural immersion.

The Joy of Independent Experiences

One of the most liberating aspects of being single is the freedom to create your own experiences. You do not have to wait for anyone to join you — you can create memorable experiences on your own.

Solo Experiences to Try:

- **Take yourself on a weekend getaway:** Plan a solo trip to a nearby city or nature spot. Wander, explore, and savour the experience of being your own travel companion.
- **Attend events or workshops:** Go to concerts, art classes, or seminars by yourself. You may even meet new people with shared interests.
- **Host a solo date night:** Cook yourself a special meal, set the table beautifully, and enjoy your own company.
- **Be spontaneous:** Take a day off and do whatever you feel like — visit a park, have brunch, or discover a new hobby.
- **Document your adventures:** Keep a journal or photo album of your solo experiences to celebrate your independence.

Finding Fulfilment Through Growth and Learning

One of the most powerful ways to cultivate joy in your solo life is by investing in *personal growth*. When you are constantly learning, evolving, and expanding your knowledge, you feel inspired and motivated.

Ways to Grow as a Single Person:

Pursue Education: Take online courses, attend workshops, or read books on subjects that fascinate you.

Develop New Skills: Learn cooking, photography, dance, or a musical instrument.

Expand Your Horizons: Visit new places, meet new people, and expose yourself to different cultures and perspectives.

Focus on Fitness: Invest in your health by building a fitness routine that makes you feel strong and energised.

Practice Mindfulness and Meditation: Use solitude as an opportunity for self-reflection and inner peace.

The Role of Friendships and Community

Being single does not mean being isolated. In fact, when you are not focused on romantic relationships, you have more time to nurture meaningful friendships and build a supportive community.

How to Cultivate Strong Friendships:

- **Host Gatherings:** Invite friends over for game nights, potlucks, or themed parties.
- **Join Groups or Clubs:** Participate in hobby groups, book clubs, or fitness classes to meet like-minded people.
- **Be Present:** Make time for your friends, listen deeply, and show genuine care.

- **Volunteer or Network:** Get involved in social or professional events to expand your connections.

Strong friendships will provide you with companionship, support, and shared experiences, enriching your solo life.

Releasing the Need for External Validation

When you build a fulfilling solo life, you stop seeking validation from relationships or external sources. You realise that you do not need a partner to feel valuable or complete. Your self-worth is no longer defined by your relationship status.

Signs You Have Cultivated a Fulfilling Solo Life:

You feel content and at peace when alone.

You pursue goals and passions with excitement.

You create joyful experiences independently.

You no longer settle for unfulfilling relationships out of loneliness.

Exercise: Craft Your Ideal Solo Day

Objective: Design a day filled with solo activities that bring you joy and fulfilment.

Instructions:

1. Imagine your perfect solo day.
    - Where would you go?
    - What activities would you do?
    - How would you treat yourself?
2. Write down a detailed plan for your solo day.

3. Make it a reality by scheduling it on your calendar.
4. Reflect on the experience in your journal afterwards.
    - Did you feel happy and fulfilled?
    - What did you enjoy the most?
    - How did it feel to create your own joy?

Repeat this exercise regularly to cultivate more happiness and fulfilment in your solo life.

Closing Thoughts

Building a fulfilling solo life is about more than just keeping busy — it is about living with *intention, purpose, and joy*. When you learn to create your own happiness, you stop seeing being single as a lack and start seeing it as a profound opportunity.

Remember:

- Your life is not on hold — it is happening right now.
- You are whole and complete as you are.
- Joy, growth, and fulfilment are available to you, regardless of your relationship status.

So, make the most of this season of your life. Discover your passions, nurture your soul, and build a life so rich with meaning that whether you are alone or with someone, you will always be fulfilled.

Worksheet

Chapter - 9
Creating Your Solo Routine – Designing A Fulfilling Daily Schedule for Yourself

"Your days are your life in miniature. When you design fulfilling days, you build a meaningful and joyful life."

The Power of a Solo Routine

When you are single, your schedule is entirely your own — an empowering freedom that allows you to design your days intentionally and meaningfully. Unlike people in relationships, you do not have to compromise your schedule or prioritise a partner's needs. Instead, you have the beautiful opportunity to craft a lifestyle that reflects your passions, values, and goals.

Creating a fulfilling solo routine is not just about keeping busy — it is about curating a daily life that nourishes your mind, body, and soul. With a thoughtfully designed routine, you can:

- Boost your productivity and achieve personal goals.
- Prioritise self-care and emotional well-being.
- Create space for passions and creativity.
- Build consistency and structure, reducing feelings of loneliness.
- Embrace joy and spontaneity while living independently.

It is essential that you learn:

- Why is having a solo routine essential for your well-being?
- How to design a balanced and meaningful daily schedule.
- Practical tips to add joy, creativity, and purpose to your days.
- Examples of fulfilling solo routines.
- How to stay flexible while honouring your unique rhythms.

1. Why a Solo Routine Matters?

When you are single, it is easy to fall into the trap of aimlessness or inconsistency, especially if your time is unstructured. Without clear goals or daily plans, you may feel unproductive, lonely, or directionless. This is why having a purposeful solo routine is so important.

Benefits of a Fulfilling Solo Routine:

Increased Productivity: A structured day helps you focus on personal goals, preventing procrastination or idle scrolling.

Improved Mental Health: Predictable routines reduce anxiety, provide stability, and boost emotional resilience.

Stronger Sense of Purpose: When your day is filled with meaningful activities, you feel accomplished and motivated.

Reduced Loneliness: Solo routines create daily rituals of joy and connection, even when you are alone.

Enhanced Self-Discipline: Following a schedule strengthens self-accountability and self-trust.

Reflection Exercise: Ask yourself:

- Do you often feel bored or unmotivated in your solo time?
- Do you lack consistency in how you spend your days?
- Are you intentional about how you use your time, or do you let the day “just happen”?

Write down your answers and reflect on whether adding more structure to your days could enhance your fulfilment.

2. Designing a Balanced and Purposeful Daily Routine

A fulfilling solo routine is not about creating a rigid schedule — it is about intentionally shaping your days to prioritise well-being, growth, and enjoyment.

Key Components of a Balanced Routine:

To design a fulfilling solo routine, aim to include these key elements:

- **Physical wellness:** Exercise, movement, and body care.
- **Mental stimulation:** Learning, reading, or creative activities.
- **Emotional self-care:** Mindfulness, journaling, or reflection.
- **Fun and play:** Hobbies, leisure activities, or spontaneous adventures.
- **Social connection:** Virtual or in-person catch-ups with friends, family, or new connections.
- **Rest and relaxation:** Time for unwinding and quality sleep.

Exercise:

Before creating your routine, write down:

- 3 priorities you want to focus on daily (e.g., fitness, creative passion, self-care).
- 2 self-care practices you want to include.
- 1 new activity you want to explore. Use these as guiding principles for shaping your daily schedule.

3. Morning Routines – Starting the Day with Purpose

How you start your morning sets the tone for the rest of the day. A purposeful morning routine boosts your mood, sharpens your focus, and creates a sense of accomplishment from the very beginning.

Components of an Empowering Morning Routine:

1. **Wake Up with Intention:**
    - Instead of snoozing, wake up with a positive intention.
    - Stretch, smile, and express gratitude for the new day.
    - Avoid checking your phone first thing.
2. **Mindfulness or Meditation:**
    - Spend 5-10 minutes in meditation or breathwork.
    - Practice gratitude by writing down 3 things you are grateful for.

3. **Physical Movement:**
    - Do a short workout, yoga flow, or morning walk.
    - Moving your body early boosts your energy and mood.
4. **Mental Stimulation:**
    - Read an inspiring book or listen to an empowering podcast.
    - Journaling or morning pages can spark creativity.
5. **Nourishing Breakfast:**
    - Prepare a healthy, enjoyable meal.
    - Enjoy it mindfully without distractions.

Sample Solo Morning Routine (1-2 Hours):

- 7:00 AM → Wake up, stretch, and express gratitude.
- 7:15 AM → 10-minute meditation or deep breathing.
- 7:30 AM → Light workout (yoga, cardio, or strength).
- 8:00 AM → Read, journal, or listen to a podcast.
- 8:30 AM → Healthy breakfast.
- 9:00 AM → Shower and start your productive day.

4. Daily Work or Productivity Block

If you work full-time, your productivity block will be largely dedicated to your career. If you have flexible hours or are self-employed, you can divide your day into productivity bursts with short breaks.

How to Stay Productive When Working Alone:

- **Time blocking:** Use 90-minute work blocks followed by 15–20-minute breaks.
- **Eliminate distractions:** Set your phone to Do Not Disturb and create a distraction-free workspace.
- **Take movement breaks:** Stretch or walk every hour to avoid sluggishness.
- **Use productivity tools:** Utilise apps like Pomodoro timers or task managers.

Solo Work Routine Example:

- 9:00 AM – 12:00 PM → Deep work session.
- 12:00 PM – 12:30 PM → Light stretching or walk.
- 12:30 PM – 1:00 PM → Lunch break.
- 1:00 PM – 4:00 PM → Productivity block (projects or tasks).
- 4:00 PM – 4:30 PM → Short break with music or mindful breathing.

5. Afternoon and Evening Routines – Balancing Work with Joy

After your workday, prioritise restorative and fulfilling activities. Use this time to recharge, learn, or explore hobbies.

Evening Routine Ideas:

Creative Expression:

- Paint, write, cook, or play an instrument.
- Engage in passion projects.

Physical Movement:

- Go for an evening walk or jog.
- Attend a dance or yoga class.

Mental Stimulation:

- Read a book or listen to a stimulating podcast.
- Explore a new skill or course.

Relaxation and Self-Care:

- Take a warm bath with soothing music.
- Practice gentle yoga or meditation.

Sample Solo Evening Routine:

- 5:00 PM – 6:00 PM: Light exercise or walk.
- 6:00 PM – 7:00 PM: Hobby or creative activity.
- 7:00 PM – 8:00 PM: Healthy dinner.
- 8:00 PM – 9:00 PM: Relaxation (meditation, journaling, or self-care).

- 9:00 PM – 10:00 PM: Read, unwind, and prepare for restful sleep.

6. Adding Joy and Adventure to Your Routine

A fulfilling solo routine is not just about productivity — it's also about creating moments of joy, spontaneity, and adventure.

Ways to Add Joy:

- Plan solo date nights (cook yourself a fancy meal or visit a new café).
- Schedule "me-time adventures" like hiking, biking, or exploring nearby towns.
- Try spontaneous activities (dance at home, try a new cuisine, or learn a new skill).

Exercise:

- Write down 3 "joy activities" you can include weekly.
- Prioritise them in your schedule.

Closing Thoughts: Your Routine, Your Freedom

Crafting a fulfilling solo routine is an act of self-love and self-empowerment. When you create a daily schedule that nourishes your mind, body, and soul, you will feel more grounded, joyful, and fulfilled — whether single or partnered.

Worksheet

Chapter - 10

Finances & Independence – Managing Money and Thriving as A Self-Sufficient Person

"Your economic security does not lie in your job; it lies in your own power to produce – to think, to learn, to create, to adapt.

(Remember I am a healer not a finance professional and these are just general advices)

Financial Independence as a Single Person

Being single offers a unique opportunity to build financial independence without the constraints or shared responsibilities of a partner. It gives you the freedom to set your own financial goals, make autonomous decisions, and create a lifestyle that truly reflects your values. However, it also comes with its own set of challenges — you are the sole breadwinner, which means every financial decision impacts your future security.

Mastering your finances is not just about surviving — it is about thriving. Financial independence empowers you to live with confidence, make choices based on freedom rather than fear, and build the life you desire. Whether you are working toward debt freedom, building wealth, or creating passive income streams, this chapter will equip you with practical strategies and financial wisdom to help you succeed.

Key Takeaways:

- Financial independence gives you freedom, security, and confidence.
- Smart money management ensures you can thrive as a single person.
- Budgeting, saving, investing, and earning are the core pillars of financial stability.
- You can build wealth, regardless of your current income, by being intentional and strategic.

1. The Power of Financial Independence – Why It Matters

As a single person, financial independence is not just a luxury — It is a necessity. When you rely solely on your own income, financial stability becomes a cornerstone of your self-sufficiency.

Why Financial Independence is Crucial for Singles:

- **Freedom of Choice:** With financial stability, you have the freedom to make bold life choices—such as travelling, changing careers, or moving cities — without being dependent on anyone.

- **Peace of Mind:** An emergency fund and stable finances provide you with security during unexpected challenges, like job loss or health issues.

- **Empowerment & Confidence:** Managing your own money and making sound financial decisions boosts your self-confidence and self-reliance.

- **Protection from Financial Vulnerability:** Without the safety net of a partner's income, financial literacy and discipline are essential.

Reflection Exercise:

- How confident do you feel about your current financial situation?

- What financial goals do you want to prioritise (e.g., debt-free living, home ownership, travel fund)?

2. Budgeting: Your Financial Blueprint

Budgeting is the foundation of financial independence. It gives you a clear overview of your income, expenses, and savings, allowing you to make informed financial decisions.

Steps to Create a Smart Budget:

- **Track Your Income & Expenses:** Write down all your sources of income and list your monthly expenses (rent, utilities, groceries, entertainment, etc.).
- **Categorise Expenses:** Divide your expenses into needs, wants, and savings.
- **Use the 50/30/20 Rule:**
    - 50% of your income goes toward essential expenses (rent, food, bills).
    - 30% toward lifestyle expenses (travel, hobbies, dining out).
    - 20% toward savings and debt repayment.
- Reduce Unnecessary Spending: Identify areas where you can cut back on expenses without sacrificing quality of life.

Exercise: Create Your Monthly Budget

- Write down your monthly income.
- List all fixed and variable expenses.
- Assign percentages for savings, spending, and essentials.

3. Saving and Emergency Funds – Your Financial Safety Net

Having savings and an emergency fund is vital as a single person. With no partner to fall back on, you need a financial cushion to handle unexpected situations, such as medical emergencies, job loss, or urgent expenses.

How to Build an Emergency Fund:

- **Set a Goal:** Aim for at least 3 to 6 months' worth of living expenses in your emergency fund.
- **Automate Your Savings:** Set up automatic transfers to your savings account every month.
- **Reduce Impulse Spending:** Redirect small, unnecessary expenses (e.g., daily coffee runs) into your savings account.
- **Keep Emergency Funds Accessible:** Store them in a high-yield savings account for easy access and growth.

Pro Tip:

- Use the "Pay Yourself First" Method—put a portion of your income into savings before paying bills or spending.

4. Managing Debt and Credit Wisely

Debt management is essential for financial independence. Reducing or eliminating debt gives you greater financial freedom and reduces stress.

Tips for Managing and Reducing Debt:

- **Prioritise High-Interest Debt:** Pay off high-interest loans or credit card debt first.
- **Consolidate Debt:** If you have multiple debts, consider consolidating them into a single, lower-interest loan.

- **Make More than the Minimum Payment:** Paying more than the minimum reduces the overall interest you will pay over time.
- **Avoid Accumulating New Debt:** Minimise the use of credit cards for non-essential purchases.

Exercise: Debt Reduction Plan

- List all your current debts, including balances and interest rates.
- Identify which debts to pay off first (start with the highest interest rates).
- Create a monthly debt repayment schedule.

5. Increasing Your Income – Multiple Revenue Streams

As a single person, relying on one source of income can be risky. Creating multiple income streams boosts your financial security and accelerates wealth-building.

Ways to Increase Your Income:

- **Freelancing or Side Hustles:** Offer your skills online like writing, design or consulting through online platforms.
- **Passive Income:** Explore opportunities like rental income, dividends, or royalties.
- **Investing in businesses:** Learn basic investing strategies to grow your wealth over time.
- **Funds or Investment plans:** Low-cost, diversified options are perfect for beginners.

Exercise: Identify New Income Streams

- Brainstorm three skills or talents you could monetise.
- Research potential platforms or markets where you could offer your services.
- Set a goal to create at least one additional income stream in the next 3-6 months.

6. Investing for the Future – Growing Your Wealth

Investing is key to long-term financial growth and security. Even small, consistent investments can build substantial wealth over time.

Simple Investment Strategies for Singles:

- **Index Funds & ETFs:** Low-cost, diversified options perfect for beginners.
- **Retirement Accounts:** Contribute to retirement plans for long-term financial security.
- **Real Estate:** If feasible, consider investing in property as a stable, long-term asset.
- **Consistent Contributions:** Commit to regular monthly contributions, even if they are small.

7. Financial Planning for the Future

Being single does not mean you should overlook long-term financial planning. Preparing for the future ensures security, stability, and peace of mind.

Key Financial Planning Steps:

- **Retirement Planning:** Contribute to retirement accounts consistently.
- **Estate Planning:** Consider drafting a will or living trust to protect your assets.
- **Insurance:** Invest in health, life, and disability insurance for financial protection.
- **Wealth Protection:** Explore strategies like diversifying your investments and minimising tax liabilities.

Exercise: Financial Vision Board

- Create a financial vision board with images, quotes, and goals representing your desired financial future.
- Include goals like debt-free living, travel, property ownership, or business ventures.

Conclusion: Financial Freedom as a Single Individual

Building financial independence as a single person empowers you to create the life you desire on your terms. With smart budgeting, saving, investing, and planning, you can enjoy a lifestyle of freedom, security, and fulfilment.

Final Thought:

"Your financial independence is the foundation of your freedom. Build it wisely, nurture it consistently, and watch it transform your life."

Worksheet

Chapter - 11
Building A Meaningful Social Life–Connection Without Clinging

"When you stop expecting people to be perfect, you can like them for who they are,"

– Donald Miller.

The Power of Healthy Connections

Being single does not mean being isolated. In fact, it provides you with a wonderful opportunity to cultivate rich, diverse, and meaningful relationships — free from the need for constant validation from a romantic partner. When you are single, you have the freedom to build a social circle that truly nourishes you, bringing companionship, joy, and support into your life.

Let us explore how to build and sustain fulfilling social connections as a single person, how to create bonds that uplift you without clinging, form genuine friendships, and nurture healthy boundaries. The goal is to surround yourself with meaningful connections that add value to your life, while still preserving your independence.

The Difference Between Loneliness and Solitude

Before diving into strategies for building your social life, it is important to distinguish between loneliness and solitude. They may seem similar, but they are vastly different experiences.

a) Loneliness:

- A sense of emptiness caused by a lack of connection.
- Often accompanied by feelings of sadness, longing, or rejection.
- Can occur even when surrounded by people, due to a lack of meaningful bonds.

b) Solitude:

- A conscious choice to spend time alone.
- Often peaceful and rejuvenating.
- Provides an opportunity for self-reflection and creativity.

Key Realisation:

You can be surrounded by people and still feel lonely, or you can be alone and feel deeply fulfilled. The quality of your connections matters more than the quantity.

Creating a Fulfilling Social Life as a Single Person

Just because you are single does not mean your social life needs to be lacking. In fact, this stage of your life offers the perfect chance to expand your social horizons and cultivate meaningful connections without the constraints of romantic obligations. Here is how:

a) Strengthening Existing Friendships:

Often, when people enter romantic relationships, they unintentionally neglect their friendships. As a single person, you have the space to prioritise and nurture these bonds.

- Schedule regular catch-ups with close friends.
- Plan fun activities together — whether it is a weekend getaway or a creative workshop.
- Be emotionally available — show up for your friends and allow them to show up for you.

Exercise:

Write down the names of 5 people you value but have not connected with recently. Reach out and schedule a catch-up. It can be a coffee date, a call, or even a virtual hangout.

b) Expanding Your Social Circle:

Being single gives you the freedom to meet new people and explore different social groups.

- **Join Clubs or Classes:** Whether it is a book club, yoga class, or dance workshop, shared interests foster genuine connections.
- **Volunteer for a Cause:** Engaging in meaningful service connects you with like-minded people while giving back to the community.
- **Attend Events or Meetups:** Look for local events, workshops, or hobby groups that align with your interests.

Exercise:

Challenge yourself to attend one new event or join a group activity this month. Push yourself slightly out of your comfort zone — it is where genuine connections often bloom.

Cultivating Deeper Connections Without Romantic Entanglement

You do not need to be romantically involved with someone to experience emotional intimacy. Platonic friendships and even casual acquaintances can provide meaningful companionship.

a) Quality Over Quantity:

- Instead of seeking to expand your social circle endlessly, focus on nurturing deeper, more meaningful relationships with fewer people.

- Prioritise connections that bring joy, support, and authenticity into your life.

b) Authentic Communication:

Deeper connections are built on open and vulnerable communication. Practice being honest about your feelings and needs with the people in your life.

- Share your thoughts and emotions openly.
- Ask thoughtful questions and actively listen.
- Be present and engaged in your interactions.

Exercise:

Choose one relationship in your life where you would like to deepen the bond. Initiate a heartfelt conversation — share something meaningful or ask about their dreams, struggles, or passions.

Setting Healthy Boundaries in Friendships

While meaningful friendships are vital, it is equally important to maintain healthy boundaries. As a single person, you may sometimes feel inclined to overcommit to friendships to avoid feeling lonely. However, overextending yourself or clinging to connections can lead to emotional exhaustion.

a) Learn to Say No:

- You do not need to accept every invitation or be available 24/7.
- Prioritise quality time over quantity of interactions.

b) Protect Your Energy:

- If you have a draining friendship, evaluate whether it is worth maintaining.
- Distance yourself from individuals who are negative, toxic, or emotionally draining.

Boundary-Setting Exercise:

Reflect on your current friendships. Identify any areas where you feel emotionally drained. Write down one boundary you need to establish. For example:

- "I will no longer engage in gossip during my time with friends."
- "I will say no to last-minute plans when I need time for myself."

Dating Without Attachment

Just because you are single does not mean you have to avoid dating altogether. However, it is important to date from a place of self-love and emotional stability, rather than seeking someone to "complete" you.

a) Date with Curiosity, Not Expectation:

- Approach dating with a sense of exploration rather than desperation.
- Enjoy the experience without fixating on the outcome.

b) Avoid Rushing into Relationships:

- Prioritise emotional connection over the need for a label.

- Do not compromise your standards out of fear of being alone.

Dating Exercise:

If you are open to dating, make 3 lists- 1 of the qualities you genuinely value in a partner, 2nd of the bad qualities you cannot tolerate in a partner and 3rd list of the grey good and bad qualities which may or may not matter.

When dating, focus on whether the person meets those standards, rather than rushing into a relationship.

Enjoying Your Own Company Amidst a Social Life

While building a social life is important, maintaining a healthy balance between socialising and enjoying your own company is essential.

- **Embrace Downtime:** Do not fill every hour with social plans. Enjoy solitude intentionally.
- **Learn to Say No:** Protect your alone time without feeling guilty.
- **Celebrate Solo Activities:** Go on solo adventures — whether it is a solo hike, a day at the beach, or a creative workshop.

Exercise:

Choose one activity you would normally do with others and do it solo. Practice being fully present and enjoying the experience.

The Ultimate Realisation – You Are Enough with or Without Others

As a single person, your connections should complement your life, not define it. A healthy social life enriches your experience but does not fill a void — because you are already whole.

Key Takeaway:

When you cultivate meaningful friendships, deepen your connections, and set healthy boundaries, you experience the joy of connection without losing your independence. You learn that companionship is beautiful, but your happiness is never dependent on it.

Conclusion:

Embracing a Balanced, Fulfilling Social Life

Being single offers you the freedom to create a vibrant, meaningful social life on your own terms. It is a chance to nurture deep friendships, explore new experiences, and enjoy authentic connections without losing your sense of self.

Final Exercise:

Write down five qualities you want in your social connections (e.g., kindness, shared values, emotional support). Use this list as your guide to building healthy, meaningful relationships.

"True connection begins with self-connection. When you are whole on your own, your social life becomes a joyful addition — not a desperate need."

Worksheet

Chapter - 12
Online Vs. Real-World Connections– Healthy Approaches to Socialising and Dating in The Digital Era

"Connection is not measured by the number of matches or likes — it is measured by the depth of authenticity."

Navigating Connection in the Digital Age

In today's world, technology has transformed the way we form and maintain relationships. Online platforms, social media, and dating apps have made it easier than ever to meet new people. However, while these tools offer convenience, they also come with challenges —

superficial connections, comparison, and even emotional burnout.

On the other hand, real-world connections offer genuine human interaction, which fosters intimacy, trust, and emotional depth. However, they may take more time and effort to cultivate.

As a single person, it is important to strike a healthy balance between online and offline socialising. Both forms of connection have their place, but relying too heavily on one can create emotional imbalances or hinder authentic relationships.

You need to learn:

- The benefits and limitations of online vs. real-world connections.
- How to approach online dating and socialising with mindfulness.
- Tips for fostering authentic real-world relationships.
- Strategies to protect your emotional well-being in the digital landscape.

1. The Rise of Digital Connection: Benefits and Pitfalls

The digital world has made it possible to connect with people across the globe with a simple swipe or click. While this accessibility has benefits, it also comes with potential downsides.

Benefits of Online Connections:

- **Convenience and Accessibility:** Dating apps and social platforms allow you to meet people outside of your immediate social circle.
- **Broader Network:** You can connect with individuals from different cultures, backgrounds, and locations, expanding your worldview.
- **Introvert-Friendly:** For those who find face-to-face interactions overwhelming, online communication provides a lower-pressure way to connect.
- **Filtering and Compatibility:** Dating apps offer filters based on shared interests, values, and relationship goals, helping you find more compatible matches.
- **Opportunities for Niche Interests:** Online groups and forums allow you to meet people who share your passions, hobbies, or lifestyle.

Pitfalls of Online Connections:

- **Superficial Interactions:** Swipe culture encourages snap judgments based on appearances, which can lead to surface-level connections.
- **Misrepresentation:** People may present idealised versions of themselves online, which can create false expectations.

- **Emotional Burnout:** Constant swiping, ghosting, or rejection can lead to emotional fatigue and cynicism.
- **Validation-Seeking:** Relying on likes, matches, or messages for validation can become emotionally draining.
- **Lack of Emotional Depth:** Digital communication lacks the nuances of in-person interaction — body language, tone, and energy—making it harder to build genuine intimacy.

Reflection Exercise: Ask yourself:

- How much of your socialising is happening online vs. in-person?
- Do you rely on dating apps or social media for validation or self-esteem boosts?
- Are your online connections leading to meaningful relationships, or are they mostly fleeting?

2. The Value of Real-World Connections

While online connections offer convenience, real-world interactions foster emotional depth, trust, and vulnerability. Meeting someone in person allows you to experience their energy, observe their body language, and build authentic rapport.

Benefits of Real-World Connections:

- **Genuine Chemistry:** In-person interactions reveal true compatibility, including physical attraction, social ease, and emotional resonance.
- **Shared Experiences:** Real-world activities — whether hiking, attending events, or exploring new places — create meaningful memories.
- **Stronger Emotional Bonds:** Face-to-face communication strengthens emotional intimacy through eye contact, touch, and shared vulnerability.
- **Better Communication:** Real-world conversations allow for clearer communication, minimising misunderstandings that often occur through text.
- **Authenticity:** People tend to present their true selves more naturally in real-world settings, making it easier to form sincere connections.

Pitfalls of Real-World Connections:

- **Limited Pool:** You may only meet people within your immediate social circles or local area.
- **Time-Consuming:** Building real-world connections requires more time and effort compared to the instant nature of online interactions.
- **Social Anxiety:** For those with social anxiety or shyness, real-world interactions may feel overwhelming.

- **Uncertainty and Rejection:** In-person interactions carry the risk of immediate rejection or awkwardness.
- **Fewer Opportunities:** If you live in a small town or have a busy lifestyle, meeting new people in-person may be more challenging.

Reflection Exercise: Ask yourself:

- Do you prioritise real-world connections, or do you rely mostly on digital platforms?
- When was the last time you made a meaningful in-person connection?
- What real-world activities or groups could you join to expand your social circle?

3. Healthy Approaches to Online Dating

Online dating is a powerful tool when used mindfully and intentionally. The key is to approach it with authenticity, patience, and self-awareness — rather than desperation or validation-seeking.

Tips for Healthy Online Dating:

- **Be Clear on Your Intentions:** Are you looking for a serious relationship, friendship, or casual dating? Being clear about your goals helps you connect with like-minded individuals.
- **Create a Genuine Profile:** Use authentic photos and write a profile that reflects your real personality, interests, and values.

- **Limit Swiping Time:** Avoid overuse of dating apps. Designate specific times (e.g., 30 minutes a day) to engage, rather than endlessly scrolling.
- **Avoid Attachment to Outcomes:** Do not invest too much emotionally in early conversations. Let connections develop gradually without attachment.
- **Prioritise Safety:** When meeting someone new, choose public places and inform a friend of your plans. Trust your instincts and prioritise your safety.

Exercise:

Review your dating app profile.

- Does it authentically reflect who you are?
- Are your photos recent and natural?
- Is your bio genuine or trying to impress?
- Do you feel excited or drained by your app usage? If it feels inauthentic, consider rewriting it with honesty and warmth.

4. Nurturing Real-World Connections

While online connections have their place, real-world socialising helps you build deeper, more meaningful relationships. Prioritising face-to-face experiences fosters emotional intimacy and enriches your life.

Ways to Build Real-World Connections:

- **Join Hobby Groups:** Take part in cooking classes, book clubs, or fitness groups where you can meet like-minded people.
- **Attend Local Events:** Go to community events, workshops, or seminars where you can engage with others.
- **Be Present in Public Spaces:** Strike up casual conversations at cafes, parks, or social gatherings.
- **Reconnect with Old Friends:** Strengthen your existing friendships by initiating get-togethers or catch-up calls.
- **Be Open to New Experiences:** Say yes to invitations and spontaneous social opportunities.

Exercise:

Set a goal to engage in one new real-world social activity every week.

- It could be attending a local event, joining a group, or inviting someone for coffee.
- Notice how it feels to interact in person.

5. Striking a Healthy Balance

To cultivate a fulfilling social life, it is essential to balance online and real-world connections. Neither should completely replace the other.

Signs of a Healthy Balance:

- You use online platforms intentionally, not compulsively.
- You prioritise real-world experiences, making time for face-to-face interactions.
- You feel energized, not drained, by your social connections.
- You are open to meeting people both online and offline. You maintain emotional boundaries with online interactions.

Closing Thoughts: Meaningful Connection in the Digital Era

In the digital age, the key to healthy socialising and dating is balance. While online platforms offer convenience, real-world interactions foster depth and authenticity.

Final Reminders:

- Authenticity matters more than convenience.
- Quality of connection outweighs quantity of matches.
- Be intentional, not impulsive, with your socialising.
- You deserve meaningful, fulfilling relationships— online or offline.

Embrace the beauty of both worlds. Let technology enhance your connections without replacing the magic of genuine, face-to-face human interaction.

Worksheet

Chapter - 13
Preparing For Future Relationships– Healing from The Past and Being Open to New Connections

*"Don't let the **past** steal your present."*

– Terri Guillemets

Opening Your Heart to Love Again

After spending time learning how to become whole and happy on your own, you may find yourself wondering, "Am I ready to love again?" For many singles, the journey of self-discovery and independence leads to a place of deeper emotional healing, making them better equipped to build healthy, meaningful relationships in the future.

However, before entering a new relationship, it is essential to heal from past wounds, reflect on old patterns, and establish a clear vision for the kind of connection you truly desire. It is essential that you go through the process of emotional healing, setting healthy boundaries, and consciously attracting compatible relationships, while maintaining your sense of freedom and self-sufficiency.

- Healing from past relationships is essential for emotional clarity and self-growth.
- Being intentional and selective helps you attract healthier, more aligned connections.
- Staying true to your personal values and boundaries ensures your well-being in future relationships.
- You can be open to love without losing yourself.

1. Healing from Past Relationships – Releasing Emotional Baggage

Before you can fully embrace new relationships, it is essential to heal the emotional wounds from your past. Carrying unresolved pain, resentment, or fear into future relationships can lead to repeated patterns, emotional triggers, and self-sabotage.

Steps to Heal from Past Relationships:

- **Acknowledge and Feel the Pain:** Allow yourself to fully feel and process any unresolved emotions from your previous relationships. Suppressing pain only prolongs the healing process.

- **Identify Patterns and Lessons:** Reflect on your past connections. What patterns do you notice? Did you accept less than you deserved? Were your boundaries crossed? Recognising these patterns prevents you from repeating them.

- **Forgive and Let Go:** Whether you were hurt by an ex or made mistakes yourself, forgiveness is key. Forgiving does not mean condoning — it means freeing yourself from the emotional grip of the past.

- **Close the Chapter with Love:** Write a "goodbye letter" to your past relationship. Express gratitude for the lessons learned and consciously release the emotional ties.

Reflection Exercise:

- Write down the emotional lessons you have learned from past relationships.

- Identify patterns of behaviour or dynamics you want to avoid in future connections.

2. Rebuilding Trust – In Yourself and Others

One of the biggest challenges after heartbreak is learning to trust again. You may find yourself questioning people's intentions or doubting your own judgment. However, rebuilding trust is possible — and it starts with trusting yourself.

Tips for Rebuilding Trust:

- **Strengthen Self-Trust:** Build confidence in your ability to make wise decisions by honouring your boundaries and listening to your intuition.
- **Release the Fear of Vulnerability:** It is natural to feel guarded after being hurt. However, staying emotionally closed off blocks new opportunities. Give yourself permission to be vulnerable again, slowly, and gradually.
- **Do not Rush:** Allow new connections to unfold slowly and organically. Rushing into intimacy too quickly can cloud your judgment.
- **Look for Consistency, Not Perfection:** Trust is built over time through consistent actions, not grand gestures.

Exercise:

Strengthening Self-Trust

- Write down three past experiences where you trusted your instincts and were right.
- Reflect on how your intuition has protected or guided you.
- This will reinforce your belief in your own ability to make sound relationship decisions.

3. Redefining Your Relationship Standards – Raising the Bar

After being single and working on yourself, you will likely have a clearer sense of your values, needs, and boundaries. Use this knowledge to redefine your relationship standards, ensuring you only attract and accept connections that align with your growth.

Setting Healthy Standards:

- **Know Your Core Values:** Identify the non-negotiables you want in a partner (e.g., kindness, emotional availability, integrity).
- **Emotional Maturity Over Chemistry:** While chemistry is important, prioritise emotional maturity, communication skills, and shared values.
- **Healthy Communication:** Ensure future partners value open, honest, and respectful communication.
- **Shared Vision:** Consider if you and your potential partner have aligned long-term goals and values.

Reflection Exercise:

- Make a list of qualities and values you desire in a partner.
- Write down past relationship red flags you want to avoid.
- This will help you recognise healthy connections and walk away from incompatible ones.

4. Keeping Your Independence in Future Relationships

While opening your heart to love again is beautiful, it is important to maintain the independence and self-sufficiency you've cultivated. A healthy relationship should complement your life, not consume it.

Tips to Preserve Your Independence:

- **Maintain Your Own Interests:** Continue pursuing hobbies, passions, and friendships independently, even in a relationship.
- **Prioritise Personal Growth:** Do not let a new relationship distract you from your self-development goals.
- **Create Healthy Space:** Allow room for both intimacy and personal space.
- **Stay Financially Independent:** Maintain your own financial stability, even if you share expenses with a partner.

Exercise:

Boundaries for Healthy Independence

- Write down three non-negotiable boundaries you want to maintain in future relationships.
- Example: "I will continue my weekly self-care rituals and personal goals, even when in a relationship."

5. Becoming Emotionally Available – Removing Walls of Protection

If you have experienced heartbreak, you may have unintentionally built emotional walls to protect yourself from future pain. While it is natural to feel guarded, staying closed off can block genuine connections.

Tips to Open Your Heart:

- **Release Fear of Rejection:** Remember that rejection is redirection toward the right person.
- **Practice Vulnerability:** Share your feelings gradually — start with small expressions of emotional openness.
- **Trust the Right People:** Be discerning, but once someone earns your trust, allow yourself to be emotionally available.
- **Live in the Present:** Do not project past relationship wounds onto new connections. Each person is unique — give them a fair chance.

Exercise:

Heart-Opening Affirmations

- Repeat these affirmations daily:
  - "I am open to giving and receiving love."
  - "I trust myself to recognize healthy connections."
  - "I am safe to be vulnerable."

6. Practising Conscious Dating – Dating with Intention

When you feel ready to date again, do so intentionally and consciously. Avoid dating from a place of loneliness or emotional neediness. Instead, date as a whole and fulfilled person, seeking a healthy connection rather than validation.

Conscious Dating Tips:

- **Clarify Your Intentions:** Are you seeking companionship, friendship, or a serious relationship? Be clear with yourself and potential partners.
- **Do not Settle:** Just because you're open to dating does not mean you should compromise your standards.
- **Stay Authentic:** Be yourself from the start. Authenticity attracts aligned connections.
- **Respect Your Boundaries:** If someone disrespects your boundaries early on, do not excusc it.

Reflection Exercise:

- Write down your dating intentions.
- Identify three deal-breakers and three relationship values.
- This clarity will help you date with purpose and self-respect.

Conclusion: Entering Future Relationships with Strength and Clarity

Healing from past relationships does not mean closing yourself off — it means loving from a place of wholeness and self-respect. As you prepare for future connections, stay true to the independent, self-loving person you have become.

Final Thought:

"Love should be a beautiful addition to your life, not a necessity. You are already whole — and the right person will complement your wholeness, not complete it."

Worksheet

Chapter - 14

Embracing Your Single Power – Celebrating Your Autonomy and Living Life on Your Terms

"Single is an opportunity to live life on your own terms, free and unencumbered."

Embrace the Power of Being Single

Being single is often viewed through a lens of lack — as though something is missing or incomplete. Society frequently romanticizes relationships, portraying them as the ultimate source of happiness and fulfilment. However, being single is not a flaw or a temporary waiting period — it is a powerful state of autonomy, freedom, and self-expression.

Learn to fully embrace your single power by celebrating your independence, living on your own terms, and creating a deeply fulfilling life. Discover how to thrive as, self-reliant individual — confident, content, and empowered in your own skin.

- Being single is an opportunity for growth, freedom, and self-actualisation.
- You can build a meaningful and joyful life without needing external validation.
- Independence gives you the power to pursue your passions, prioritise your well-being, and live authentically.
- You are complete and whole on your own.

1. Reframing the Single Narrative – From Lack to Liberation

For too long, being single has been associated with loneliness, inadequacy, or incompleteness. In reality, being single offers extraordinary freedom and empowerment. It is a time when you can truly put yourself first without compromise.

Shifting Your Perspective:

- From “Alone” to “All One”: Instead of viewing singleness as being “alone,” see it as being “all one” — whole, complete, and self-sufficient.

- Freedom, Not Limitation: Without the responsibilities of a relationship, you have the freedom to prioritise your personal growth, passions, and goals.
- No Need for Validation: When you learn to validate and fulfil yourself, you are no longer dependent on others for emotional stability or happiness.

Reflection Exercise:

- Write down all the positive aspects of being single that you genuinely enjoy (e.g., freedom, flexibility, self-discovery).
- Anytime you feel disheartened about being single, refer back to this list to remind yourself of the gifts it offers.

2. Embracing Your Independence – Living on Your Terms

One of the greatest joys of being single is the ability to live life entirely on your own terms. You have the freedom to make decisions based on your own desires, values, and goals.

Ways to Celebrate Your Independence:

- **Create Your Own Schedule:** You have the freedom to structure your days and routines exactly as you want. You can prioritise your passions without having to accommodate a partner's needs.

- **Pursue Solo Adventures:** Whether it's travelling alone, exploring new hobbies, or attending events, being single allows you to be spontaneous and adventurous.
- **Set Your Own Boundaries:** You have the power to define your own boundaries — whether with family, friends, or colleagues — without the constraints of a partnership.
- **Financial Freedom:** When you're single, you have complete control over your finances. You can save, invest, or spend according to your priorities.

Exercise:

Designing Your Ideal Single Life

- Imagine you have complete freedom to design your ideal life.
- Write down how you would spend your days, who you would surround yourself with, and what experiences you would prioritise.
- Use this as a blueprint for creating your most fulfilling single life.

3. Prioritising Self-Care and Well-Being

When you are single, you have the luxury of focusing entirely on your own well-being. This is a time to nurture your mind, body, and soul without compromise.

Self-Care Practices for Singles:

- **Emotional Self-Care:** Journaling, therapy, or engaging in self-reflection practices strengthens your emotional well-being.
- **Physical Self-Care:** Prioritise regular exercise, nourishing meals, and restful sleep. You have the freedom to create health rituals that suit your preferences.
- **Spiritual Self-Care:** Practice meditation, yoga, or other spiritual rituals that help you connect with yourself.
- **Creative Self-Care:** Engage in creative outlets like painting, writing, or dancing. Express yourself freely without needing external validation.

Reflection Exercise:

- Create a self-care schedule for the week.
- Include practices that nurture your physical, emotional, and spiritual well-being.

4. Pursuing Your Passions & Purpose

Being single provides you with uninterrupted time and energy to explore your passions and pursue your life's purpose. This is the perfect opportunity to dive into creative endeavours, educational pursuits, or career ambitions.

Tips for Cultivating Your Purpose:

- **Reconnect with Old Dreams:** Rediscover hobbies or passions you may have set aside.
- **Learn New Skills:** Take classes, learn a language, or develop skills that excite you.
- **Volunteer or Give Back:** Contributing to causes you care about gives your life meaning and fulfilment.
- **Focus on Career Growth:** Without the emotional demands of a relationship, you can fully commit to your professional goals.

Exercise:

Purpose Discovery Journaling

- Write down the activities or causes that make you feel most alive.
- Reflect on how you can incorporate more of these into your daily life.

5. Building a Fulfilling Social Life

Just because you are single does not mean you have to be socially isolated. In fact, being single offers you the chance to cultivate a diverse and fulfilling social life.

Tips for Strengthening Your Social Circle:

- **Nurture Friendships:** Invest time in meaningful friendships. Plan regular meetups, game nights, or weekend adventures.

- **Join Interest-Based Groups:** Connect with people who share your passions and interests, whether through sports, art, or book clubs.
- **Be Open to New Connections:** Attend events or classes where you can meet like-minded individuals.
- **Embrace Solo Social Activities:** Go to movies, concerts, or museums alone — it can be surprisingly liberating and enjoyable.

Exercise:

Expanding Your Social Circle

- Write down three social activities you'd like to try.
- Make plans to attend them solo or with friends.

6. Celebrating Your Single Milestones

You do not need a partner to celebrate personal milestones and achievements. Honour your individual journey by marking your own victories.

Ways to Celebrate Your Achievements:

- **Create Single-Specific Traditions:** Treat yourself to special outings, gifts, or experiences when you reach a goal.
- **Celebrate Independence Day:** Pick a day each year to celebrate your singlehood with self-love rituals or fun activities.

- **Honour Your Growth:** Acknowledge the emotional and personal growth you have achieved during your single journey.

Reflection Exercise:

- Write a list of personal milestones you have achieved as a single individual.
- Celebrate your growth, resilience, and independence.

7. Recognising That You Are Already Whole

The most powerful realisation of all is that you are already whole — regardless of your relationship status. Your worth is not defined by your relationship status, but by your authenticity, self-love, and fulfilment.

Affirmations for Wholeness:

- "I am complete and whole just as I am."
- "My happiness comes from within."
- "I embrace my single power with joy and confidence."

Exercise:

Daily Affirmation Practice

- Repeat these affirmations every morning to reinforce your sense of self-sufficiency.

Conclusion: Thriving as an Empowered, Independent Soul

Being single is not just a phase — it is a powerful chapter of self-discovery, independence, and freedom. It is a time when you learn to love yourself deeply, pursue your dreams, and embrace life on your own terms.

Final Thought:

"Being single is not about waiting for someone to complete you — it's about becoming so complete that you inspire the right person to join your beautiful, whole journey."